...S AND
...UFF

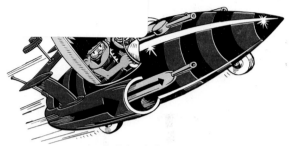

By Deborah Chancellor
Designed by Gary Cookson
Cover design by Ch'en-Ling

KINGFISHER
An imprint of Larousse plc
New Penderel House
283-288 High Holborn
London WC1V 7HZ

First published by Larousse plc 1998

2 4 6 8 10 9 7 5 3 1

ISBN 0 7534 0182 7

KING*f*ISHER

2

3

THE UNIVERSE

The universe is huge! Astronomers think it contains about 100 billion galaxies, with 100 billion stars in each one. Even the fastest spaceship would take 100 million years to reach the nearest star.

TRAVELLING LIGHT

We measure how far away a star is by the time its light takes to reach us. Light travels at 300,000km per second. Light from Proxima Centauri, the nearest star to our Sun, takes 4.2 years to reach Earth. It is 4.2 light years away.

BIRTH OF THE UNIVERSE

Astronomers think a massive explosion gave birth to the universe. They call this event the Big Bang. Hot dust and gases were blasted in all directions, forming the galaxies and stars.

Big Bang

Since the Big Bang, galaxies have been moving outwards.

HOW OLD IS THE UNIVERSE?

The universe is still expanding with the force of the Big Bang. Astronomers can measure the speed that galaxies are moving outwards, so working backwards, they reckon that the universe began fifteen billion years ago.

Time Chart

Event	Time
Modern civilization	Now
Humans appear	4.5 million years ago
Life on Earth begins	4 billion years ago
Solar system forms	5 billion years ago
Stars develop	11 billion years ago
Galaxies form	14 billion years ago
Big Bang	15 billion years ago

No-one knows where all the material to make up the universe came from in the first place.

GALAXIES

A galaxy is a huge collection of stars, held together in space by a powerful pulling force called gravity. Separate galaxies group together in 'clusters' – gigantic groups of these clusters form 'superclusters'.

GALAXY SHAPES

There are four different kinds of galaxy: spiral, elliptical, barred spiral and irregular. Planet Earth is in a galaxy called 'The Milky Way', which is a spiral galaxy. If seen from above, it would look like an enormous whirlpool, with long, spiralling arms. The Milky Way is made up of over 100 billion stars, and is so named because at night we can sometimes see part of it looking like a band of milky white light across the sky. The Milky Way is in a cluster of up to 30

A spiral galaxy

A barred spiral galaxy

An elliptical galaxy

galaxies, called 'The Local Group'. This cluster contains several spiral, irregular and elliptical galaxies.

OUR LOCAL GROUP

Light takes five million years to cross from one side of our 'Local Group' of galaxies to the other. This may seem huge, but it is in fact quite small compared to some other galaxy clusters. The 'Virgo Cluster' is made up of about 1,000 galaxies, and is twenty million light years across.

AMAZING ANDROMEDA

Andromeda is the largest galaxy in the 'Local Group'. Our own Milky Way comes second. Light from Andromeda takes two million years to reach us. This means that we never see what the galaxy looks like now – we only see what Andromeda looked like two million years ago, when mammoths walked the Earth.

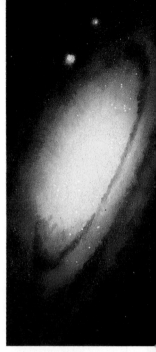

Millions of galaxies have now been identified including Andromeda.

BALLOON UNIVERSE

1 Paint galaxy shapes close together all over a large balloon.

2 Let the paint dry, then blow up the balloon to see how the galaxies are moving apart as the universe expands.

THE MILKY WAY

We live on a globe called Earth, which is one of nine planets travelling round the Sun. Earth is not a particularly big planet, and the Sun is only one of 100 billion stars in our galaxy, the Milky Way.

Earth travels around the Sun, a star at the edge of our galaxy.

STAR CITY

Just under half of the stars in the Milky Way are grouped in the middle of the galaxy, and we can see some of them in the night sky, but there are many, many more which we can't see. The whole galaxy is named after this city of stars, and is called 'The Milky Way'. At the centre, are old stars that formed with the galaxy about fourteen billion years ago. The spiralling arms contain vast clouds of gas and dust, where new stars form. The Milky Way is always producing new stars – one is born approximately every 18 days.

SPINNING SPIRAL

From above, the Milky Way looks like a catherine wheel, with arms winding outwards from the centre. Stars in the galaxy are always moving, as

The Milky Way looks like two fried eggs back to back. In the middle, the nucleus, there are ancient red giant stars. Some astronomers think a giant black hole may lie at the centre.

the spiral slowly spins round. Our solar system takes 225 million years to make a complete circuit of the spiral – this is called a 'cosmic year'. Since it was formed, our galaxy has completed this circuit 52 times. One cosmic year ago, dinosaurs roamed the Earth.

FLOATING FREE

As well as rotating, the Milky Way is racing through space at a speed of some 2.2 million kilometres per hour.

BIG BULGE

Seen from side on, the Milky Way bulges out in the middle, like two fried eggs back to back. This 'bulge' of stars

measures 20,000 light years from top to bottom.

WHERE ARE WE?

Our solar system is about two-thirds of the way out from the centre of the Milky Way. If you could squeeze the solar system into a teacup, the rest of the Milky Way would be as big as North America.

The Milky Way, as seen from the Earth.

9

THE SUN

Did you know the Sun is a star? It doesn't look like one because it is so close compared to other stars – the Sun's light only takes eight minutes to reach us. Without the Sun's light and warmth, there would be no life on Earth!

HOW HOT IS THE SUN?

Never look directly at the Sun, because its heat and light is blinding. The Sun's diameter is 109 times bigger than Earth's. Nuclear reactions at the heart of this huge fireball reach temperatures of up to fifteen million °C. The outside of the Sun is a lot cooler, reaching temperatures of just 6,000°C. But even this is still 25 times hotter than the hottest kitchen oven!

The Sun's surface is burning and constantly moving.

LOSING WEIGHT

The Sun burns off four million tonnes in weight and uses the equivalent of more than thirty million truck loads of fuel every second; just think how much lighter it is since you started reading this page! Still, the Sun has so much mass that it won't burn out for at least another five billion years. The Sun's surface is often dotted with spots and eruptions, or 'flares'.

The Sun's gravity holds the planets in orbit.

Sun

Orbit

Planet

Sometimes, enormous looping arches of gas, known as 'prominences' can be seen rising from the Sun's surface.

STRUCTURE OF THE SUN

There are five layers of burning gas around the Sun's core. Together, their weight

stops the nuclear reactions in the Sun's core running out of control.

THE SOLAR SYSTEM

The planets move around the Sun in oval-shaped orbits, spinning as they go. The Sun's gravity keeps them in their orbits and controls their spin. There are four inner planets (Mercury, Venus, Earth, Mars) and five outer planets (Jupiter, Saturn, Uranus, Neptune, Pluto).

The word planet comes from the Greek word Planetes which means wanderer.

13

MERCURY AND VENUS

Mercury and Venus lie between the Earth and the Sun. Mercury is nearest to the Sun, and Venus is our closest neighbour. Mercury and Venus are both rocky planets. Mercury is covered in craters, while Venus has some of the tallest mountains in the solar system.

Earth

Mercury

WHAT A DAY!

A planet's year is the time it takes to orbit the Sun. Mercury has the shortest year of all the planets, only 88 Earth-days long. A planet's day is the time between two sunrises. On Mercury, one day is 176 Earth-days long, so its days are longer than its years!

PLANET OF EXTREMES

Mercury is so close to the Sun, that its long days are

Mercury's surface

Earth

Venus

scorching hot, reaching up to 350°C. This small planet has no atmosphere to trap heat, so by night the temperature drops down to −170°C.

IS VENUS LIKE EARTH?

Venus is the same size as Earth, but you wouldn't want to go there! Venus has:

- A poisonous carbon dioxide atmosphere, with orange clouds of sulphuric acid.
- A runaway greenhouse effect which makes it the hottest planet, with temperatures of up to 480°C – almost five times as hot as boiling water.
- A crushing surface pressure, 90 times greater than Earth.

During 1990-92, the Magellan spacecraft mapped 99% of Venus' surface.

EARTH AND MOON

The Earth and Moon are partners – the Moon orbits the Earth and both orbit the Sun together. Seen from the Moon, Earth looks blue, because two-thirds of it is covered in water. The Moon is rocky and dry. In 1969, the first astronauts landed on the Moon.

Earth

LIFE ON EARTH

Earth is the only planet in the universe that we know to have life. The gases in the Earth's atmosphere protect us from the Sun's harmful rays. The Earth's surface is always changing, making life possible.

NEW MOON

Soon after the solar system formed, a huge planet may have crashed into Earth. Hot liquid rock 'splashed' into space, hardening to form the Moon. Meteorites then crashed on its surface making craters.

STRANGE SILENCE

The Moon has no atmosphere, so there is no air to breathe. It is completely silent and still. Footprints made by the astronauts will stay there for millions of years, as there is no wind to blow the dust away.

Earth's structure

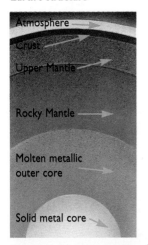

Atmosphere
Crust
Upper Mantle

Rocky Mantle

Molten metallic outer core

Solid metal core

MOON WALK

Walking on the Moon is easier than on Earth! The Moon's gravity has less power to pull you downwards, so you would be six times lighter on the Moon than you are on Earth.

Moon

EARTH BIRTH

The solar system was born when a huge cloud of gas and dust in space began to shrink and spin. The middle of the cloud heated up to form the Sun. Dust packed together in the rest of the spinning cloud, making the balls of rock we call planets.

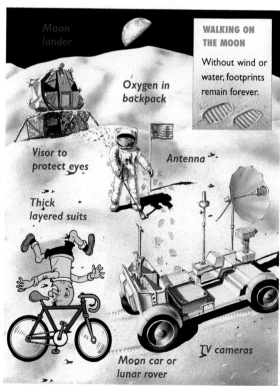

Moon lander

Oxygen in backpack

Visor to protect eyes

Thick layered suits

Antenna

WALKING ON THE MOON

Without wind or water, footprints remain forever.

Moon car or lunar rover

TV cameras

MARS

Of all the planets, Mars is most like our own, but it is farther away from the Sun, so is much colder. There is frozen water vapour in the atmosphere, and Mars has ice-capped poles.

Mars

the planet reflects the Sun's light, so from Earth, Mars looks red. Red dust in the atmosphere turns the Martian sky pink.

FLYING POTATOES

Mars has two moons, called Phobos and Deimos. Shaped like potatoes, they are no bigger than cities. They were probably once asteroids, pulled into orbit around Mars by the planet's gravity.

THE RED PLANET

A long time ago, water flowed on Mars. It reacted with iron in the soil to make the rocks go rusty! The rocky surface of

TALL AND DEEP

The largest volcanic mountain on Mars is called Olympus Mons. It is 26km high – three times the size of Everest – and has a crater the size of London. A canyon on Mars called the Mariner Valley is so long, it would stretch from one side of the USA to the other.

LIFE ON MARS?

People used to think they could see canals and vegetation on Mars, but in 1976, the Viking space probes found nothing of the sort. Perhaps life existed on Mars when the planet had water. A Martian meteorite has been found dating back to this time, which hints at the possibility of life.

The largest volcano in the solar system is found on Mars. It is called Olympus Mons and is 500km wide at its base.

Space probes have been sent to Mars to see if there are any living things there. So far, nothing has been found.

JUPITER

Jupiter is the biggest planet in our solar system. Despite its giant size, Jupiter spins round in under 10 hours, making it bulge in the middle. Jupiter is five times farther from the Sun than the Earth.

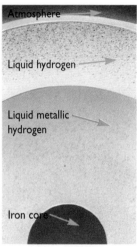

Atmosphere

Liquid hydrogen

Liquid metallic hydrogen

Iron core

Jupiter does not have a solid surface, but consists of gases around a solid core.

HARD CORE

The rocky core at the heart of Jupiter is the same size as Earth, but 20 times heavier. It reaches temperatures of up to 30,000°C, and is covered with an ocean of liquid hydrogen 1,000km deep.

POISONOUS ATMOSPHERE

Thick, colourful clouds of poisonous gases make up Jupiter's atmosphere. They are blown around the planet by winds of up to 500km per hour. Jupiter's 'Great Red Spot' is a spectacular hurricane, three times the size Earth.

JUPITER'S MOONS

Jupiter has 16 moons. Some of the most interesting are Io, Europa and Ganymede. Io is covered with active volcanoes which can shoot material

Earth

Jupiter's ring

Jupiter

Great red spot

200km into space before it falls back to the surface, icy Europa is as smooth as a billiard ball, and Ganymede is the biggest moon in the solar system, measuring 5,262km across.

The Galileo space probe was launched in 1989 and reached Jupiter in December 1995.

MISSION ACCOMPLISHED

The Galileo space probe reached Jupiter in 1995. One part went into orbit around the planet, and the other entered the atmosphere, working for almost an hour before losing contact. It sent back information about Jupiter's atmosphere.

The Great Red Spot is the only permanent feature on the ever-changing surface of Jupiter. It has been observed by astronomers for hundreds of years.

SATURN AND URANUS

It would be impossible to land on Saturn or Uranus, because, like Jupiter, these planets do not have solid surfaces. Saturn and Uranus are huge gas planets. Both are circled by rings and a number of moons.

RINGS OF ICE

Saturn is a beautiful planet. Its rings are made of pieces of ice, some as small as specks of dust and others as big as houses. The rings are 275,000km in diameter, but are only 10km thick.

MANY MOONS

Saturn has 20 moons, the most of any planet in the solar system. Titan is the most unusual – it has very dense air, but is far too cold for life with a temperature of just −180°C. It is sometimes called 'an Earth in deep freeze'.

FLOATING BALL

Even though Saturn is 95 times heavier than Earth, its material is very loosely packed and it is the least dense planet. It would float like a beach ball in a vast ocean of water.

Earth

Saturn

Saturn's ring

DISCOVERING URANUS

Uranus was discovered in 1781 by William Herschel. He was fascinated by astronomy and studied the skies with a home-made telescope.

BLACK RINGS

Uranus' rings are under 10km wide. They are difficult to see, because the boulders in them are made from some of the blackest material in the solar system.

TILTED ORBIT

Uranus orbits the Sun on its side, possibly due to a collision with another planet or large body. Each pole gets 42 years of continual darkness followed by 42 years of constant sunlight.

Saturn's rings are made up of billions of particles.

Sunlit pole

Uranus

Pole in darkness

NEPTUNE AND PLUTO

Neptune and Pluto are the coldest planets, because they are farthest from the Sun. Neptune is gassy and big, but rocky Pluto is the smallest and lightest planet. It is also the faintest, only discovered by telescope in 1930.

Methane gas, which reflects blue light, gives Neptune its distinctive colour.

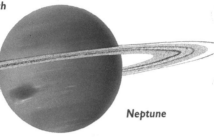

Neptune

COLD AND BLUE

Neptune was discovered in 1846. Its freezing temperature drops to -210°C. Neptune's largest satellite, Triton, has the

Atmosphere of hydrogen, helium and methane

Mantle of ice

Iron core

Pluto's orbit

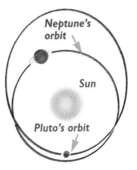

Neptune's orbit

Sun

Pluto's orbit

coldest land surface in the solar system. Its crust of rock-hard ice is -235°C.

PLUTO'S ORBIT

For 20 years of its orbit, Pluto travels closer to the Sun than

Neptune is a giant gassy planet with an iron core.

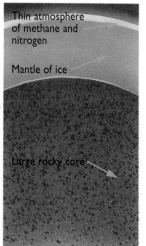
Pluto

orbit its planet backwards. Pluto's moon is half the size of Pluto, which makes it the biggest moon compared to its planet.

BAD WIND

Neptune has the fastest winds in the solar system. They blow around its 'Great Dark Spot' at up to 2,000km/h.

Neptune. Between 1979 and 1999, Neptune is farthest from the Sun. Pluto has the longest year of any planet, taking 248.5 years to circle the Sun.

STRANGE MOONS

Triton, one of Neptune's moons, is the only moon to

Thin atmosphere of methane and nitrogen

Mantle of ice

Large rocky core

PLANET X

Astronomers think there may be a planet beyond Pluto. They know something is affecting the orbit of Uranus and Neptune, but Pluto is not big enough to do this by itself. Perhaps space probes will discover another planet, 'Planet X' as they travel out of the solar system.

Tiny Pluto has a large rocky core surrounded by ice.

29

SPACE ROCK

Planets are not alone in the solar system. Also circling the Sun are asteroids and comets. Meteors, or 'shooting stars', are small pieces of rock that burn up in the Earth's atmosphere. Chunks of rock that are too big to burn are called meteorites. If these crash to Earth, they can cause enormous damage.

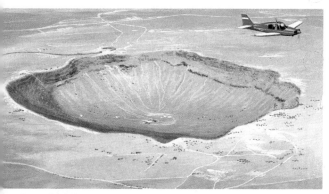

Some 24,000 years ago, a meteorite hit the Arizona desert with the force of 1,000 Hiroshima-sized atomic bombs.

ASTEROID BELT

Asteroids are lumps of rock and metal, some as big as planets. A belt of about 45,000 asteroids exists between Mars and Jupiter. The asteroid Psyche is made of pure iron – useful for building space stations on or near Mars!

HALLEY'S COMET

Comets are balls of ice and rock with shining 'tails' of hot gas and dust. One of the most famous is Halley's comet, which can be seen from Earth every 76 years. Each orbit, it loses 250 tonnes of material; at this

The Old Woman meteorite weighs 2,758kg. It was found in 1976.

rate, it will last another 170,000 years.

COMET CLOUD

Some comets have very long orbits,

Comets are like huge dirty snowballs in space. They consist of loose rock and dust welded together by frozen gas.

An especially bright meteor is called a fireball.

such as the McNaught-Russell comet, last seen in 1993 which will not return for another 1,550 years!

Meteors usually burn up at a height of about 50km above the Earth.

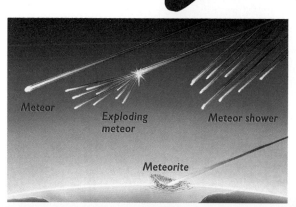

Meteor

Exploding meteor

Meteor shower

Meteorite

THE LIFE OF A STAR

The night sky is studded with stars, ranging from the very young to the very old. Astronomers study stars of all ages, to work out how they are born, what happens during their lives and how they die.

LIFE STORY

A cloud of dust and gas, called a 'nebula' gives birth to a 'star'. The star shines, burning up its energy. When all the energy is used up, the star shrinks inside, but the outside swells and cools to become a 'red giant'. Finally the outer part is thrown off, leaving a small core. This 'white dwarf' shines weakly till it dies.

Cloud of gas and dust

Star contracts

Star expands

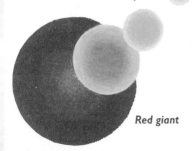

Red giant

White dwarf

EXPLODING STARS

A very big star collapses in a huge explosion called a 'supernova'. For a few days or weeks, the blast sends out the power of 100 million suns. It leaves behind a patch of gas (raw material for a new star) and the core of the dying star.

HEAVY STARS

The core of a dying supernova is called a 'neutron star'. These stars are about the size of a city (10km across) and are extremely heavy. One pinhead of a neutron star weighs as much as the QEII. Some neutron stars spin and send out radiation – they are called 'pulsars'.

BLACK HOLES

When a star over eight times bigger than our Sun dies, it becomes a 'black hole', collapsing with such force that it pulls everything around in with it. Not even light can escape.

Crab Nebula

The Crab Nebula is a huge cloud of gas. Sometimes the gas forms rings.

Ring Nebula

A star that gets too close to a black hole get sucked into it. Not even light can escape the pull of the black hole's gravity

SEEING STARS

Groups of bright stars in the sky are called 'constellations'. There are 88 constellations, named, after people, gods and animals from ancient times. The northern world has a different pattern of stars to the southern world.

CHANGING IDEAS

People used to think that the Earth was the centre of the universe. Astronomers in the 14th and 15th centuries proved that the Earth and other planets revolved around the Sun. Now we know that our solar system is a speck in just one of billions of galaxies.

PRECISION VISION

For centuries, astronomers used simple hand-held telescopes to study the stars. Today, the world's largest and most powerful telescopes could see a car's headlights from 25,000km away.

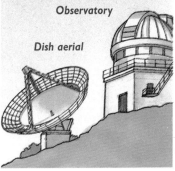

Giant telescopes collect light from space. Most are in observatories in mountain peaks. Dish aerials pick up radio waves from space.

Observatory

Dish aerial

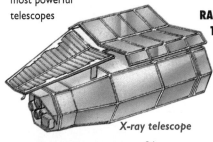

X-ray telescope

RADIO TELESCOPES

Invisible radiation from distant stars, and radio signals from space probes, can be

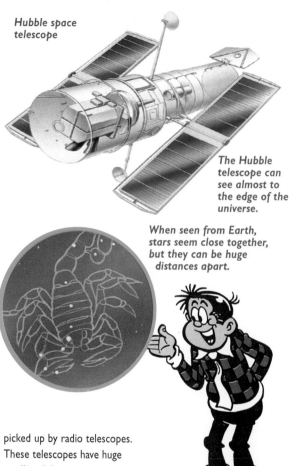

Hubble space telescope

The Hubble telescope can see almost to the edge of the universe.

When seen from Earth, stars seem close together, but they can be huge distances apart.

picked up by radio telescopes. These telescopes have huge satellite dishes to receive such messages.

SPACE TELESCOPE

The problem with telescopes on Earth is that images are distorted by the atmosphere. In 1990, the Hubble telescope was placed in orbit 600km above Earth. It can see objects 50 times fainter and seven times farther away than any telescope on Earth. It is able to see millions of distant galaxies.

SPACE TRAVEL

Space travel is extremely expensive and must be carefully planned. If a space mission is too long or dangerous for astronauts, space probes are sent. Probes have explored all the planets except Pluto, the most distant planet.

MOON MISSIONS

Only 12 astronauts have ever walked on the Moon. There is now new interest to explore the Moon, to mine the rich minerals in its soil. In the future, bases could be set up on the Moon, as springboards for farther space travel.

Space shuttle

SPACE SHUTTLE

The space shuttle is economical, as most of it can be reused. It launches like a rocket, with the power of 140 jumbo jets, flies like a spacecraft and lands like a plane, at 350km per hour. The shuttle is used to launch and repair satellites, and take astronauts to space stations.

FUTURE SPACE TRAVEL

In the future, large 'supershuttles' could be used to ferry passengers from Earth to orbiting space cities. Scientists are now working on a space plane, which could reach 25 times the speed of sound and fly from London to Sydney in just two hours.

Rockets launch into space at 40,000km/h, the speed needed to escape from Earth's gravity.

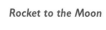

The Apollo rockets carried astronauts to the Moon and back.

IS ANYONE OUT THERE?

Somewhere in space, there could be life on a distant planet. It would be so far away, that it would take many lifetimes to get there. Our most distant space probe, Pioneer 10, is now travelling beyond the solar system. It carries information about

Earth and humans to give to any space travellers it may meet!

Astronauts use backpacks, called MMUs, to move outside their spacecraft.